**NATIONAL
GEOGRAPHIC**

Glass

Robyn Crocker

Contents

Amazing Glass

Glass is an amazing material. It has many features that make it useful. Glass is **transparent**, or see-through. Glass windows let light in. They also let us see outside. People make jars and bottles out of glass. You can see what is inside glass jars without having to open them.

▼ The girl can see the cookies through the glass.

Glass is easy and inexpensive to produce. Think of all the different things that are made of glass. Our world would be very different if we didn't have glass.

We eat and drink out of ▶ glass cups and dishes.

▲ Glass light bulbs light up the dark.

▲ Eyeglasses help many people see better.

▲ We use glass
test tubes when
we do science
experiments.

▲ We watch
television on
screens made
of glass.

▲ We look through glass windows.

5

The History of Glass

People have used glass for thousands of years. Long ago, people used a rock called **obsidian** to make spear tips. Obsidian is a kind of natural glass. It is made when sand is melted by the extreme heat of a volcano.

This knife was made from ▶ obsidian thousands of years ago.

▼ When lava from a volcano melts sand, it makes obsidian.

No one knows for sure when and where glass was first made. Glass beads have been found in the graves of people who lived about 4,000 years ago. The first glass bowls, cups, and bottles were made about 3,500 years ago.

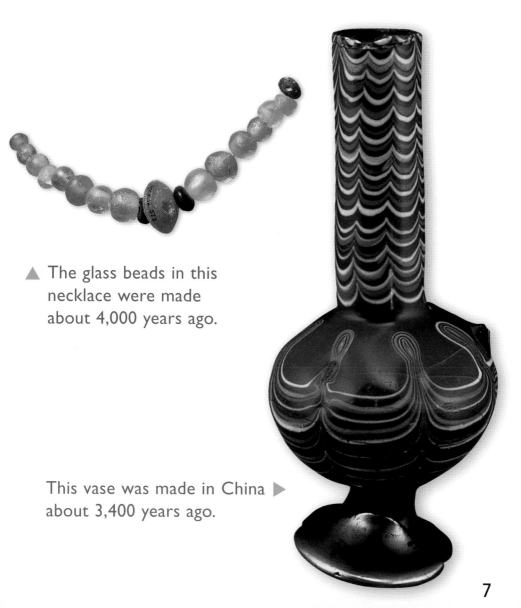

▲ The glass beads in this necklace were made about 4,000 years ago.

This vase was made in China ▶ about 3,400 years ago.

About 2,000 years ago, people used glass to make many different things. They made glass plates, cups, jugs, and vases. They also made flat glass that could be used for windowpanes.

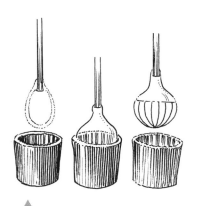

▲ People made glass objects by blowing into hot glass that had been placed into a mold.

Making Glass Today

Most glass is made in factories. Silica, which is a mineral found in sand, and other ingredients are mixed together. They are heated in a **furnace**, which is a huge oven. This mixture melts, or becomes **molten**, in the furnace. The molten glass is used to make many different kinds of glass objects.

▼ The ingredients used to make glass are melted in a furnace.

Molded Glass

Bottles and jars are made using molten glass and molds. A mold is a hollow container. The molten glass is cut into sections called **gobs**. One gob is put into each mold. Air is blown into the mold to spread the glass into its shape.

▼ These bottles are taking their final shape.

The bottles and jars are then removed from the molds. They are put into a long oven called a **lehr**. The bottles are heated again and cooled slowly. Reheating the glass makes it stronger.

▲ This glass and container were made using molds.

Flat Glass

Windows, doors, and mirrors are made out of flat glass. To make flat glass, a ribbon-shaped piece of molten glass is floated on a bath of hot liquid metal. The glass then passes along rollers in a lehr where it is cooled slowly. Then the flat sheets of glass are cut into different sizes.

▲ The molten glass comes out of the furnace in the shape of a ribbon.

The walls of this building are made with flat glass. ▶

Glassblowing

Some glass objects are made by blowing glass. Glassblowing is a way of making glass objects that has been used for over 2,000 years. Glassblowers make beautiful glass objects in different shapes, sizes, and colors.

The glassblower dips a long, thin metal tube into molten glass to pick up a gob of glass. He or she blows gently into the other end of the tube. The air makes the gob of glass form a hollow **bulb**. The glassblower keeps turning the pipe to stop the bulb from drooping. When the bulb has been blown to the right size, it can be pushed into the correct shape and cut.

Air is blown into ▶ the molten glass to make it hollow.

Once the bulb
is the right size,
it can be shaped.

Recycling Glass

Sometimes glass can be used more than once. Some types of glass can be **recycled** or made into other glass objects. Glass that can be recycled is collected and taken to a recycling factory.

▼ Glass is crushed before it is recycled.

At the recycling factory, colored glass is separated from clear glass. Then all the glass is cleaned. Finally it is crushed until it looks like gravel. The crushed glass goes to the glass factory. Only a few types of glass are recycled.

What Can Be Recycled?

Can Be Recycled	Can't Be Recycled
✔ clear, green, and brown glass bottles and jars	✗ broken window glass ✗ broken windshields ✗ heat-resistant glass ✗ vases ✗ television screens ✗ light bulbs ✗ mirrors

Different Kinds of Glass

There are many kinds of glass. Each kind of glass is made in a different way. Each kind of glass does a special job.

Safety Glass

When safety glass breaks, it crumbles into small pieces that are not sharp. Many types of windows are made from safety glass. Some basketball backboards are made from safety glass. Bullet-proof windows and airplane windshields are made from extra strong safety glass.

▼ This basketball backboard is made from safety glass.

Optical Glass

Optical glass is used in telescopes, microscopes, and eyeglasses. It is made with a curved or rounded surface. Optical glass can make distant and tiny things easier to see clearly.

▼ This piece of glass will be used inside a huge telescope.

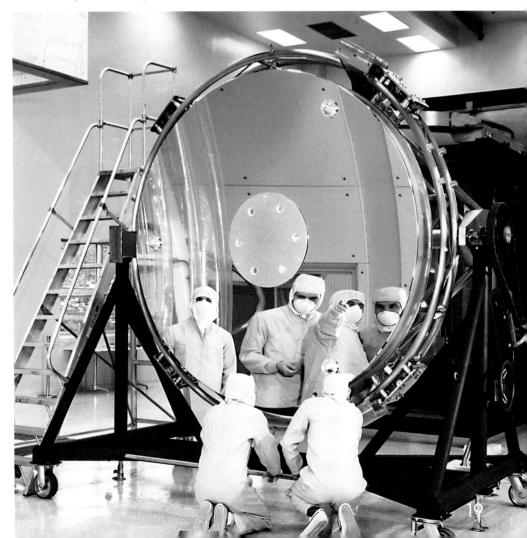

Fiberglass

Fiberglass is very different from other kinds of glass. It is thin fibers of glass that can be finer than human hair, but stronger than steel. Fiberglass is made by stretching molten glass until it is very long and thin. It's so thin that it can bend without breaking!

▼ Molten glass is stretched to make fiberglass.

◀ A man installs fiberglass insulation in a house.

▼ This small boat is made out of fiberglass.

Fiberglass has many uses. It is used as **insulation** in houses. It keeps homes warm in winter and cool in summer. Some firefighters' suits are made from fiberglass. Plastic is mixed with fiberglass to make safety helmets, boats, car parts, ropes, and surfboards.

Conclusion

Think about all the ways we use glass. Today, glass is used to make many things. It has been used to make useful and beautiful things for thousands of years. Glass is an amazing material.

▼ You can easily see what's in glass jars.

Glossary

bulb   a rounded hollow gob of glass that a glassblower shapes

furnace   an oven where glass can be heated to very high temperatures

gob   lump of molten glass

insulation   material used to keep houses warm or cool

lehr   a long oven used to reheat and cool glass

molten   melted using heat

obsidian   a kind of natural glass

recycled   something new made out of something old

transparent   see-through

Index